AF428234

WHAT IS AN ASTRONAUT?

Astronomy Book for 9 Year Old
Children's Astronomy & Space Books

What are astronauts, and what do they do? Let's find out about this exciting, dangerous job, and meet some of the most famous astronauts.

STAR-SAILORS

When nations began to plan to send people into space, they had to come up with a title for these people. The Soviet Union developed the term cosmonaut, which means "cosmic voyager". The United States National Aeronautics and Space Administration (NASA) preferred astronaut, which means "sailor among the stars". Most of the world now uses astronaut to speak about the men and women who have rocketed from Earth into orbit around it, and even to visit the Moon.

AN ASTRONAUT IN SPACE

ASTRONAUTS
Discovery

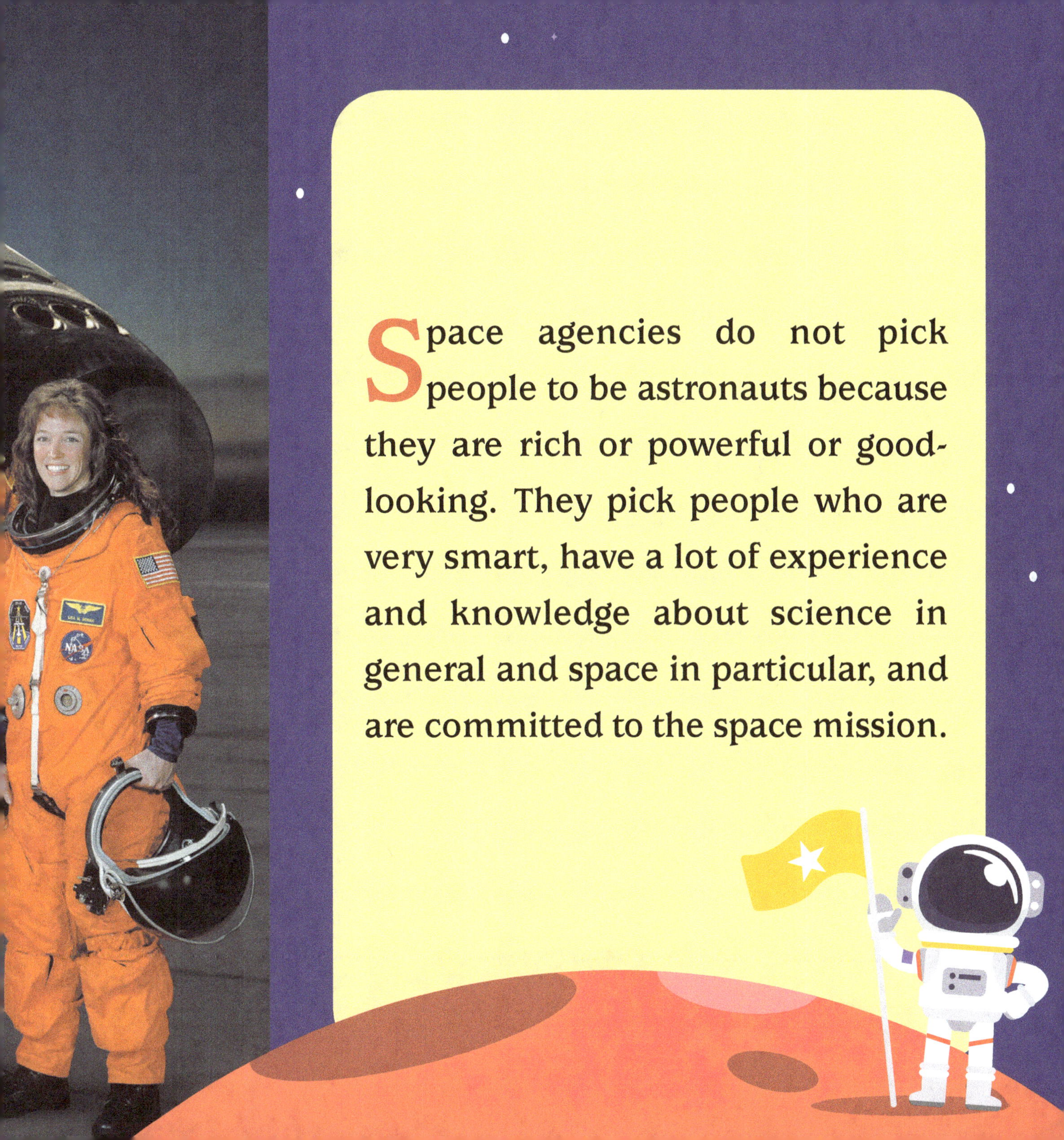

Space agencies do not pick people to be astronauts because they are rich or powerful or good-looking. They pick people who are very smart, have a lot of experience and knowledge about science in general and space in particular, and are committed to the space mission.

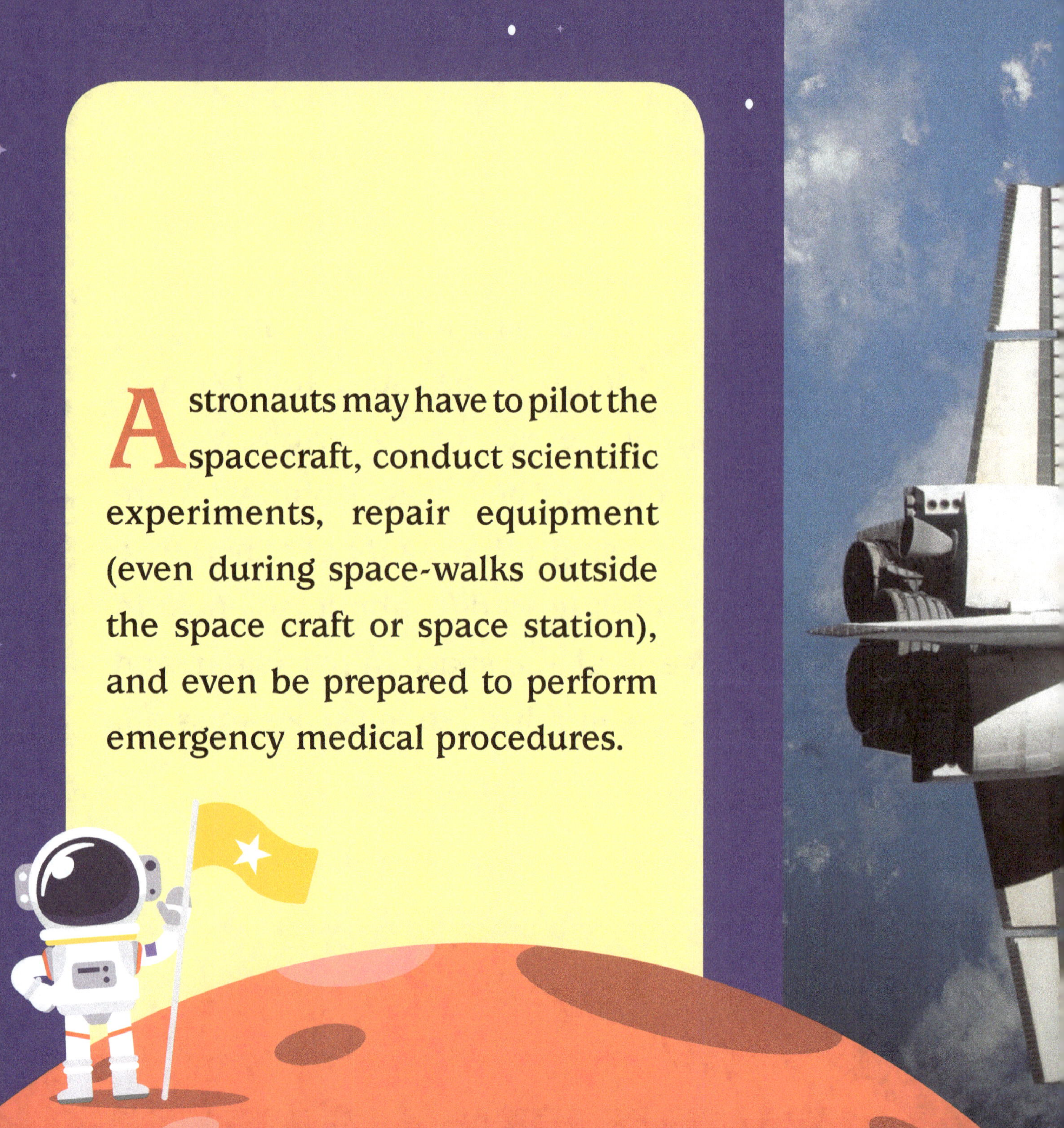

stronauts may have to pilot the spacecraft, conduct scientific experiments, repair equipment (even during space-walks outside the space craft or space station), and even be prepared to perform emergency medical procedures.

SPACE SHUTTLE ENDEAVOUR IN ORBIT

SALLY RIDE
Once an astronaut is selected, he or she enters a multi-year training program.

NASA, and the space agencies of other countries, train their astronauts for their complicated and dangerous work

WHAT ASTRONAUTS DO

The earliest astronauts' job was mainly to survive. The first spacecraft were to get the astronaut into space for a trip of a few hours and back home again, but had very little by way of research equipment or supplies.

NASA ASTRONAUT GROUP 18

SPACE SHUTTLE COLUMBIA'S CREW
BROWN CLARK CHAWLA ANDERSON RAMON HUSBAND MCCOOL
STS 107

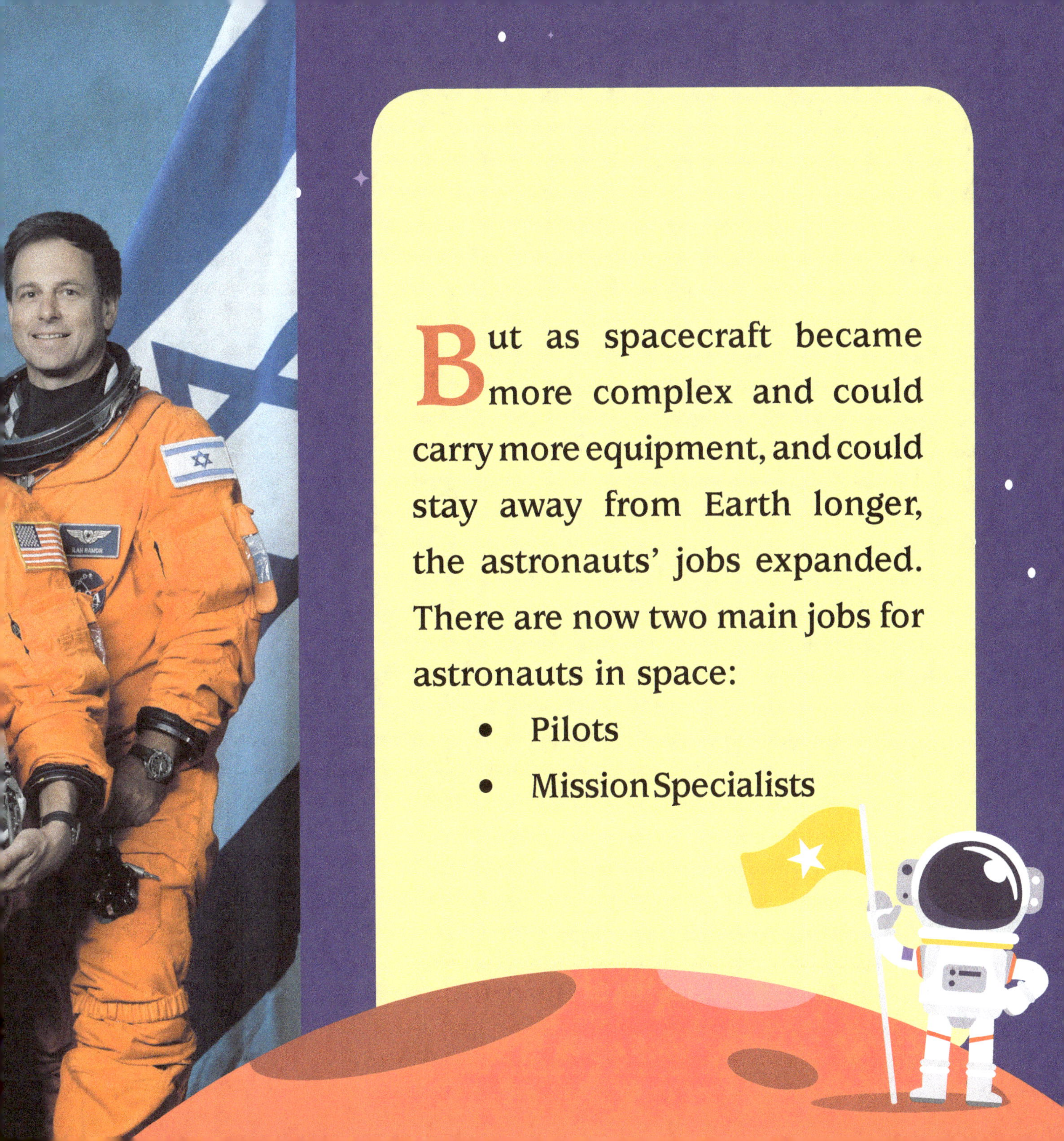

But as spacecraft became more complex and could carry more equipment, and could stay away from Earth longer, the astronauts' jobs expanded. There are now two main jobs for astronauts in space:

- Pilots
- Mission Specialists

Pilots: pilot astronauts control spacecraft like the now-retired Space Shuttle, the Soyuz space capsule, and the International Space Station (ISS).

They are like the captains of a ship, responsible for the success of the mission, the survival of the crew, and bringing their craft safely to its destination.

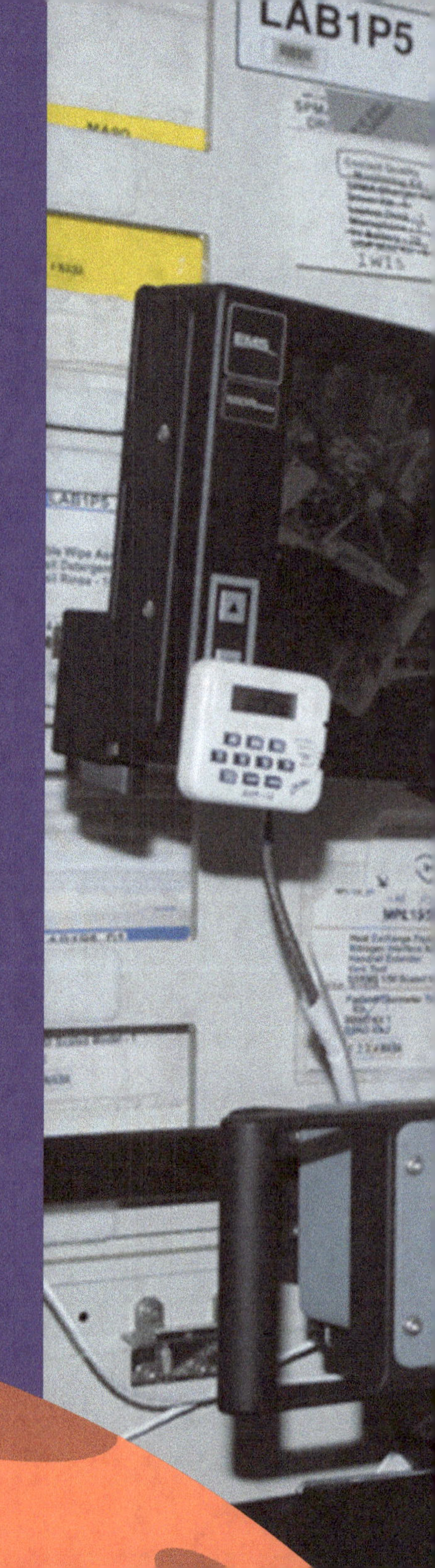

Mission specialists: The rest of the crew are mainly trained in special scientific and technical areas. They conduct experiments, launch and repair satellites, keep the ISS running, and even act as doctors to other crew members. They have to be able to do these things in weightless conditions, in cramped space, with limited tools, and often while wearing a spacesuit!

OCHOA, STS-110 MISSION SPECIALIST, WORKS THE CONTROLS OF THE CANADARM2 IN THE DESTINY LABORATORY

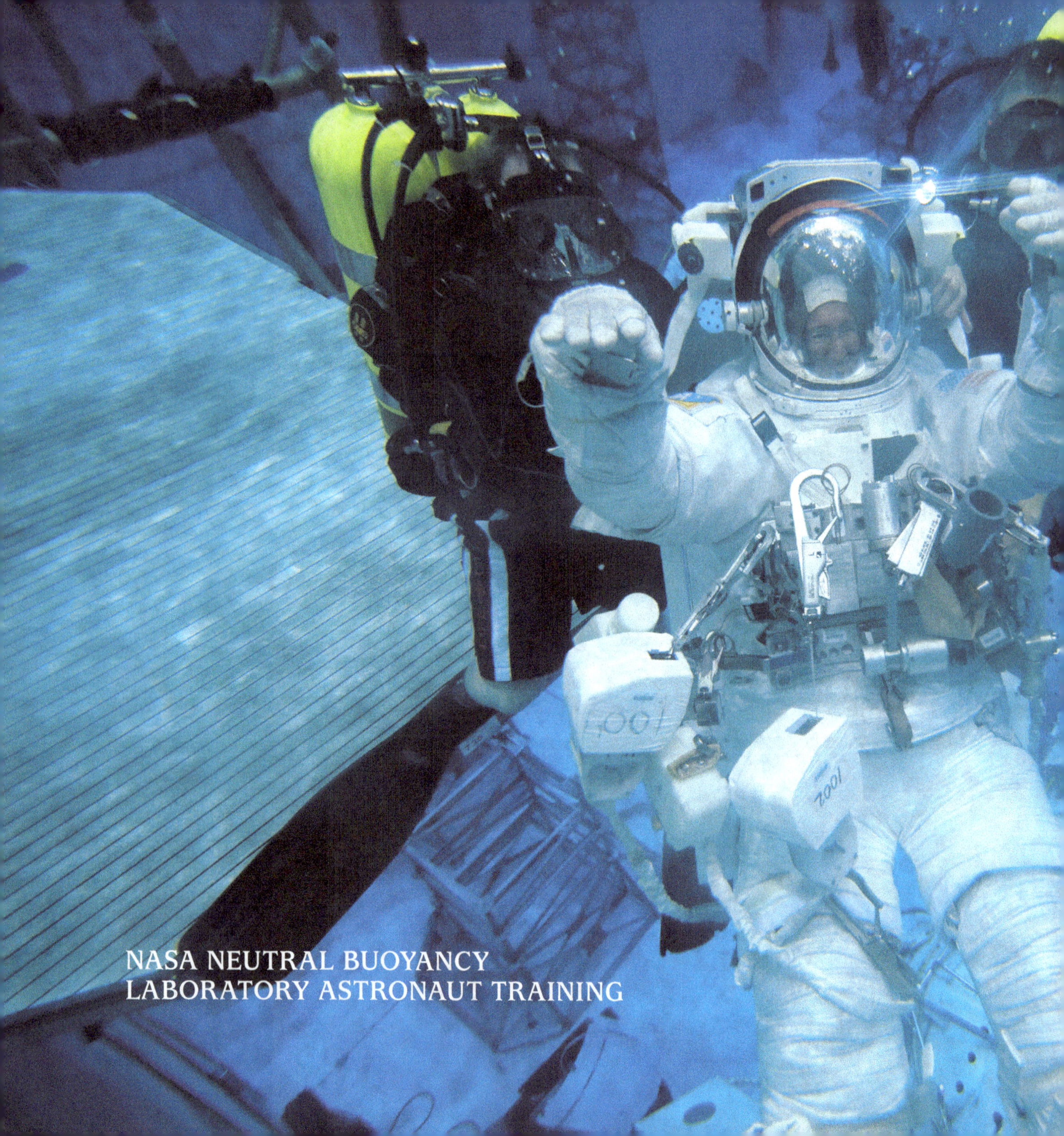

NASA NEUTRAL BUOYANCY
LABORATORY ASTRONAUT TRAINING

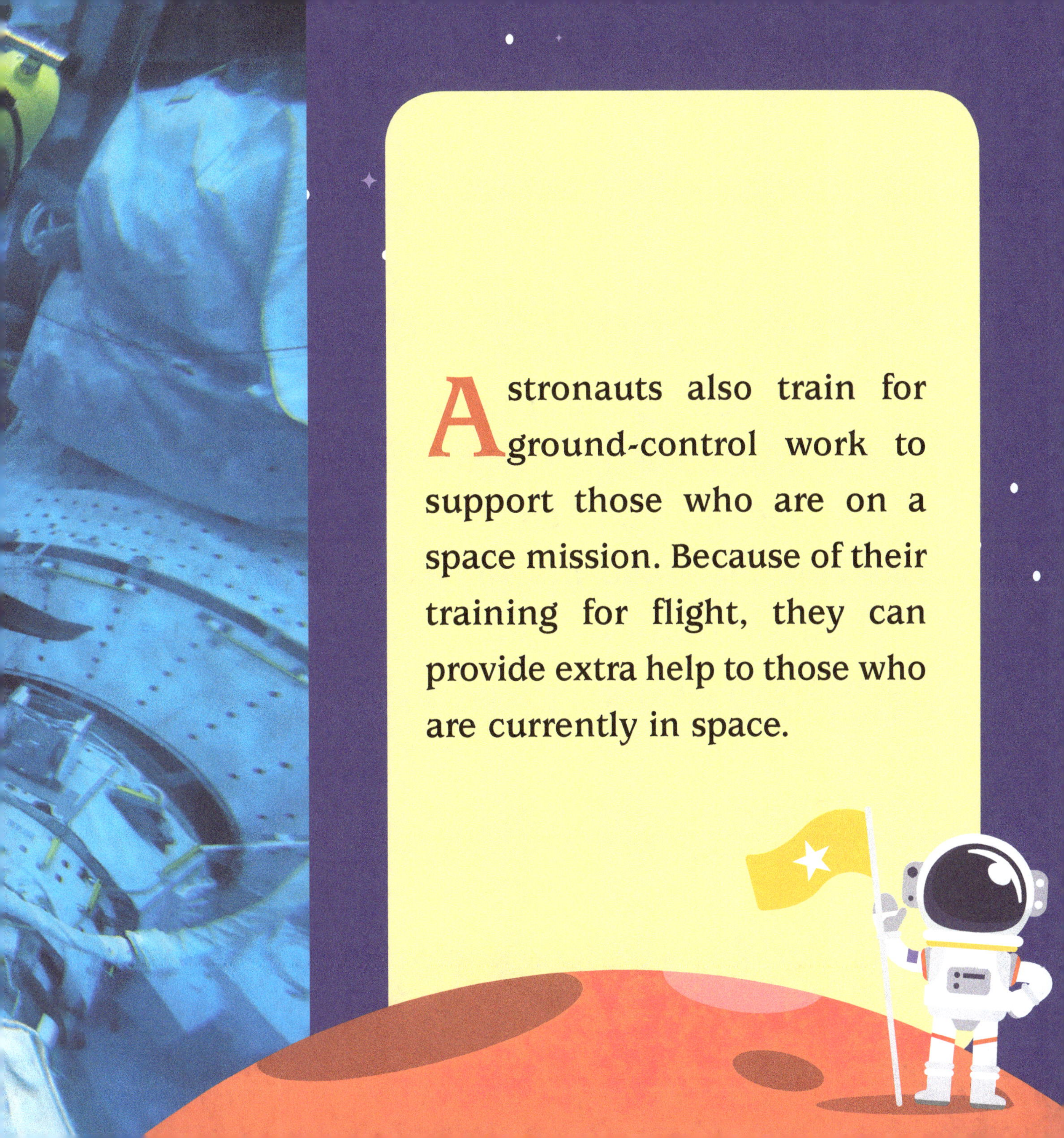

Astronauts also train for ground-control work to support those who are on a space mission. Because of their training for flight, they can provide extra help to those who are currently in space.

Astronauts also learn to be good public speakers, so they can explain to the world what is happening in space and why space programs are important. This helps develop support for space programs so governments continue to provide funds, and helps recruit new astronauts.

APOLLO 11 ASTRONAUT BUZZ
ALDRIN SPEAKS TO MEMBERS
OF THE NEWS MEDIA

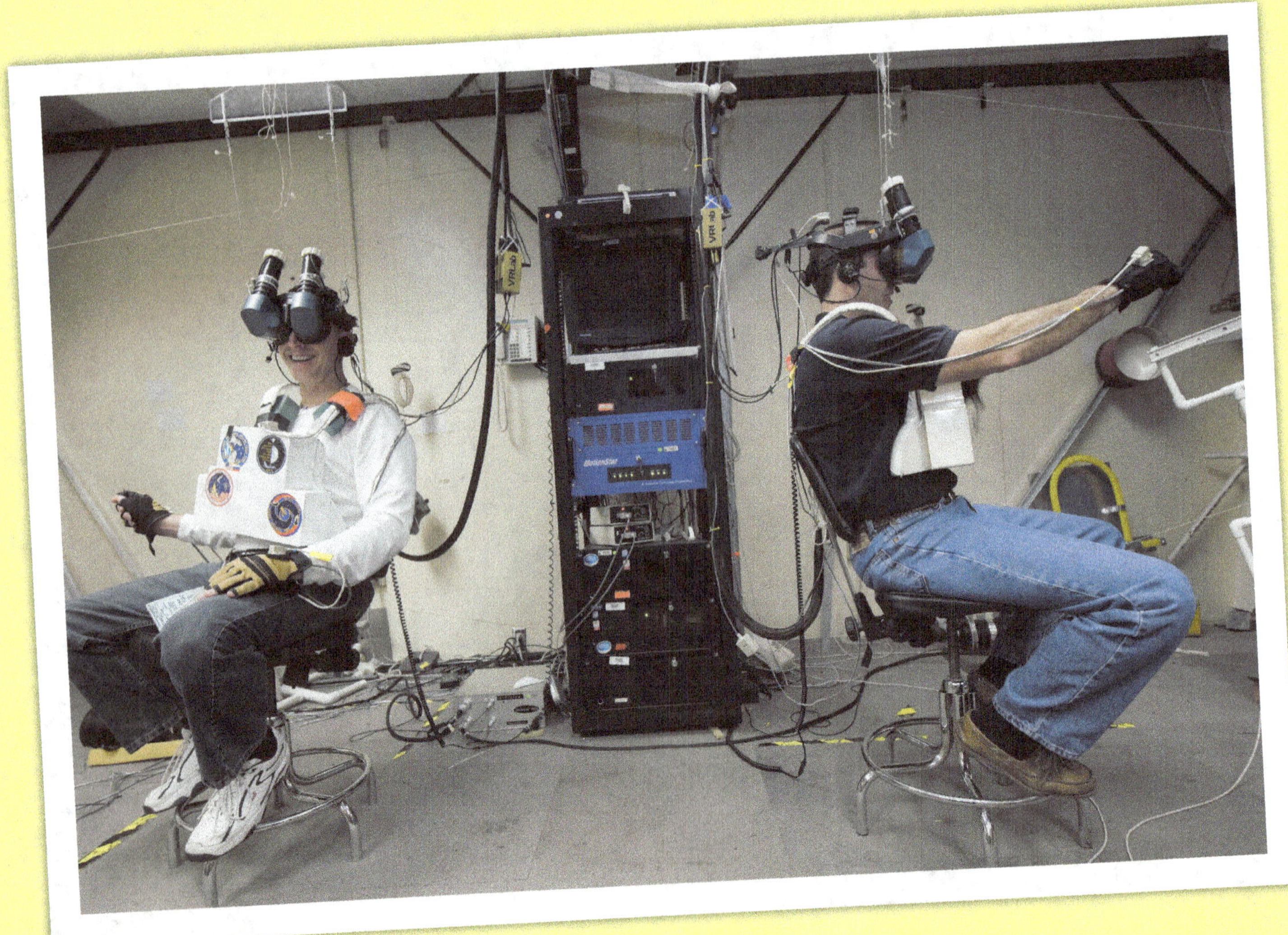

TRAINING SPACE VEHICLE MOCK-UP FACILITY

HOW ASTRONAUTS TRAIN

Training for astronauts covers several areas: astronauts have to be physically fit, up to date on everything in their field of specialization, be at least competent in at least one other field, and know their spacecraft and how to keep it running the way they know their own homes.

They also have to learn to be very good at teamwork and at not being distracted or depressed by the risks and limitations of where they are working.

Almost one thousand people have taken astronaut training, mainly with the Johnson Space Center in Texas, or at Star City, near Moscow in Russia. The training has several phases, and trainees who do not do well may have to leave the program.

TRAINING SHUTTLE MISSION SIMULATOR 1

BASIC TRAINING

Astronaut basic training lasts about two years. Trainees learn the space vehicles they may be using, and about the systems of the ISS. In classrooms, they study meteorology, space science, engineering, and some earth sciences. The trainees arrive with a lot of knowledge in many areas, and those who complete basic training are like one-person university science departments!

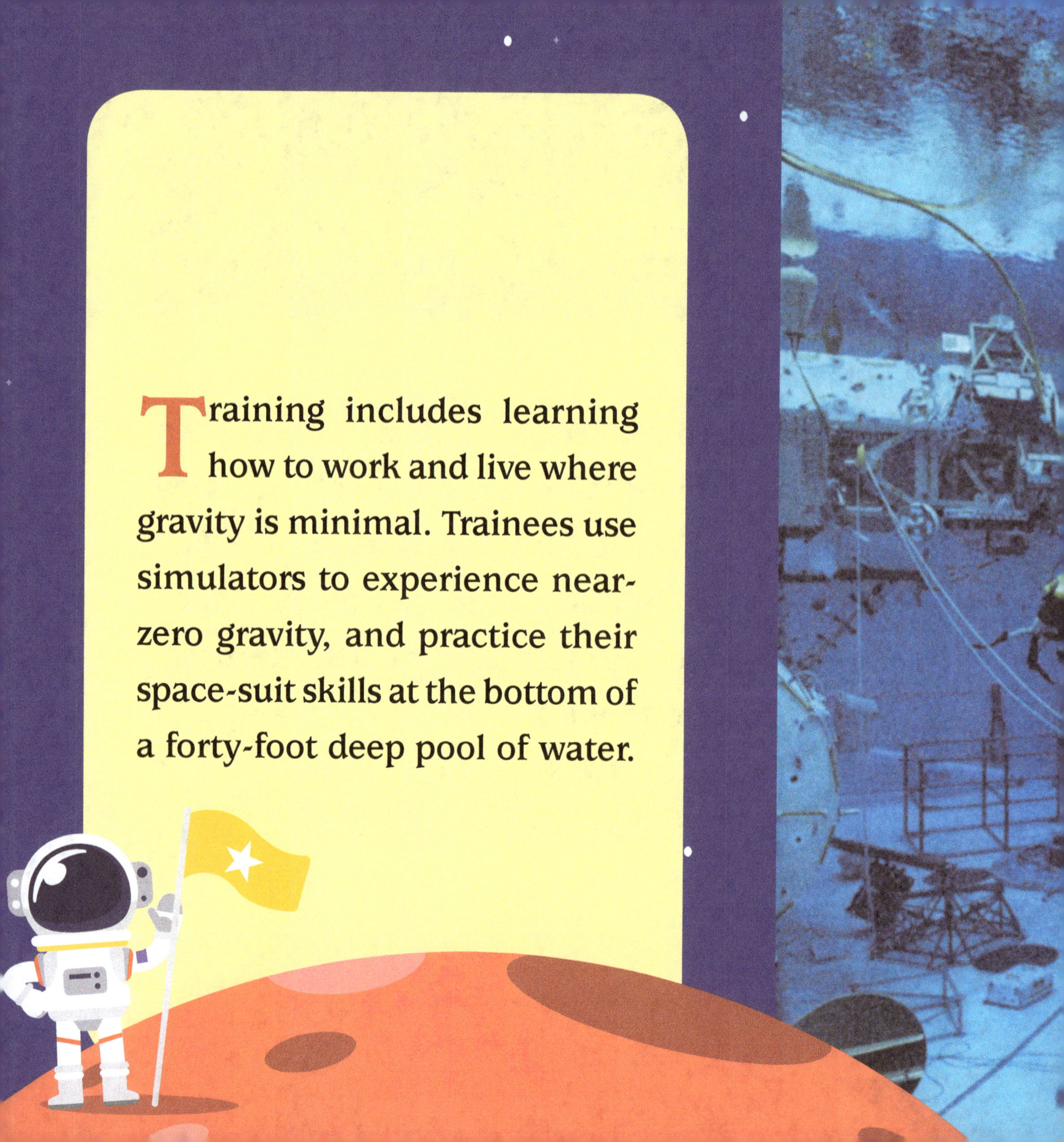

Training includes learning how to work and live where gravity is minimal. Trainees use simulators to experience near-zero gravity, and practice their space-suit skills at the bottom of a forty-foot deep pool of water.

UNDERWATER EVA SIMULATION

BASIC SURVIVAL TRAINING

Basic training includes survival training. This is not so much for what the astronauts might meet in space, but for what they might meet when they get back to Earth. If their spacecraft lands in water, they have to be able to swim and tread water and stay afloat until they can be rescued. Most ISS crew members return to earth in a Soyuz space craft that lands on the ground in Russia, and future space craft, such as the vehicles being designed by Space-X, may make the return to Earth even less dangerous. However, astronauts still complete survival training, just in case!

SECOND-PHASE TRAINING

Trainees who complete basic training may be invited to enter the second phase. They can start calling themselves astronauts now, even though they have not yet been off Earth.

NASA
MCDONNELL
GEMINI
WEIGHTLESS TRAINING

MIGHTY FIRE FALCONS '89
AIR FORCE
AIR FORCE
OVHD
EXIT
EMERGENCY EGRESS DRILL ON-BOARD TRAINING

Experienced astronauts work with the new recruits on every type of activity they may have to do, in pre-launch, the launch of the vehicle, orbiting the Earth or docking with ISS, conducting experiments or maintenance while in space, working in a space suit, and getting back to Earth.

MISSION TRAINING

The final phase is for the astronauts who are selected for a specific mission. For instance, if you are selected to become part of the ISS crew for a mission lasting several months, you will get the good news almost a year before you can expect to launch into space. The next ten months focus on two things:

- Peak Condition
- Mission Tasks

ASTRONAUT AIRMAN LAUNCHED

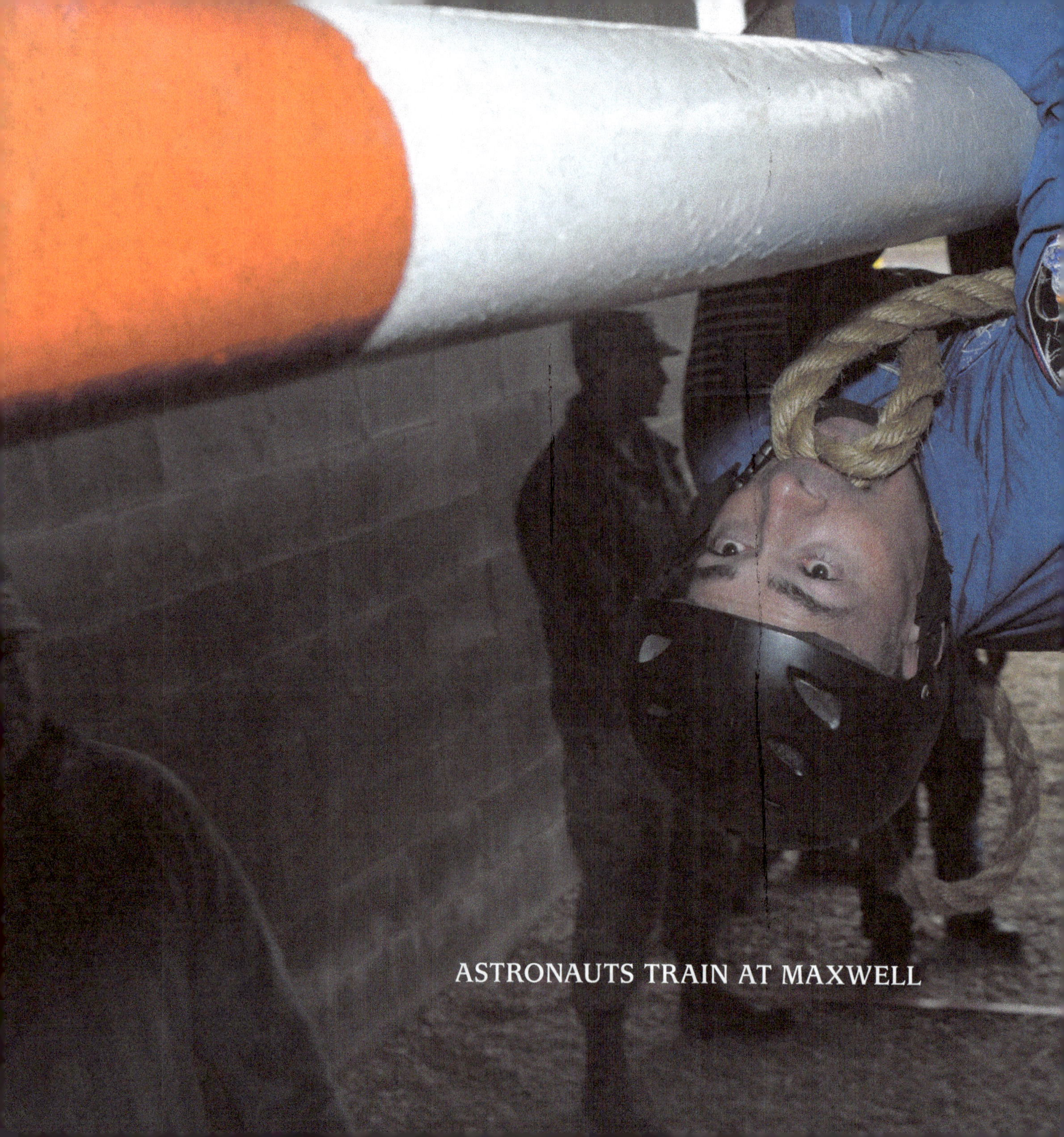
ASTRONAUTS TRAIN AT MAXWELL

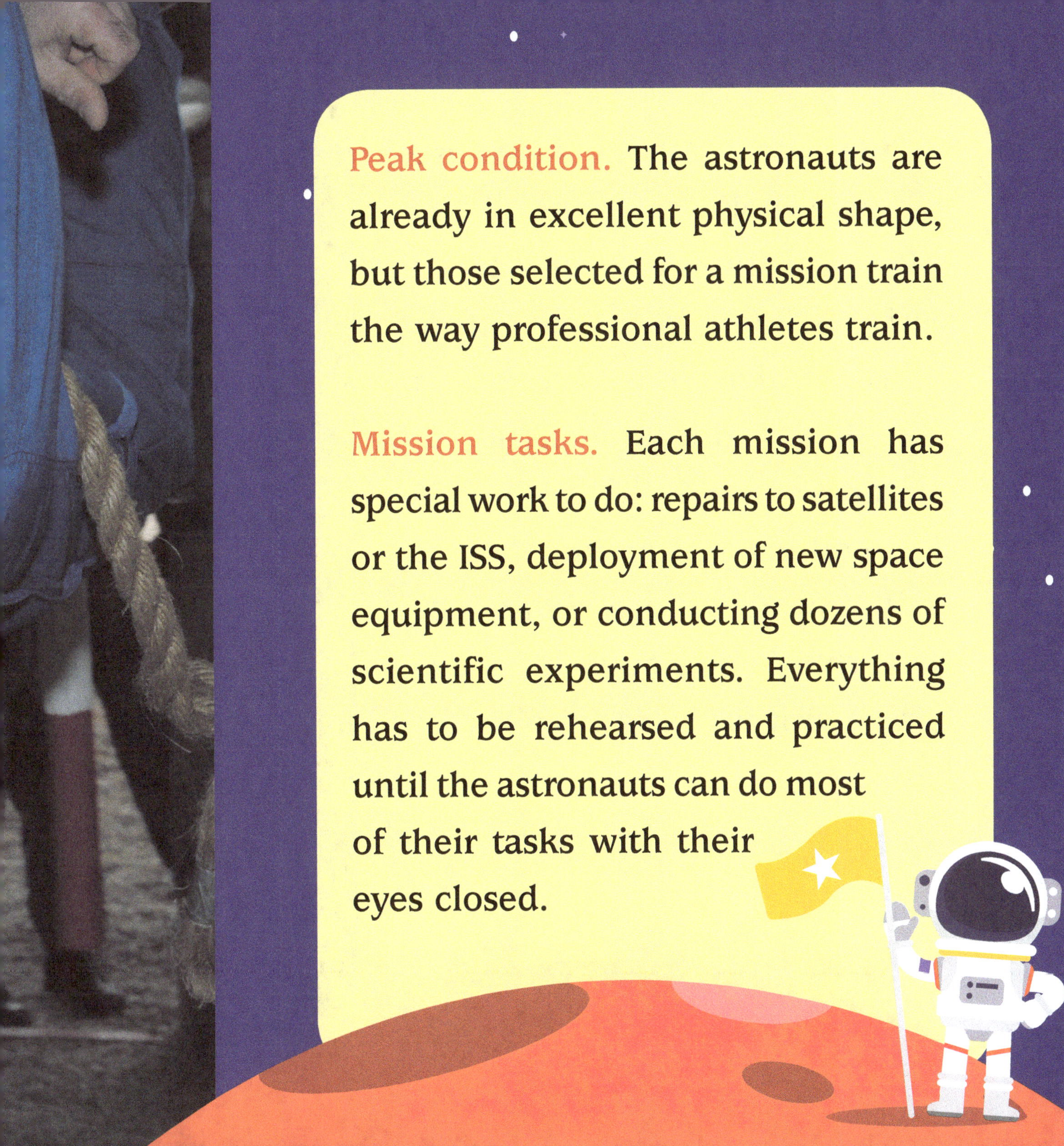

Peak condition. The astronauts are already in excellent physical shape, but those selected for a mission train the way professional athletes train.

Mission tasks. Each mission has special work to do: repairs to satellites or the ISS, deployment of new space equipment, or conducting dozens of scientific experiments. Everything has to be rehearsed and practiced until the astronauts can do most of their tasks with their eyes closed.

The mission tasks may involve new tools that none of the mission team have ever worked with before, with scientific concepts that only experts in that field really understand, or unstable or fragile materials. And if something goes wrong, there is no hardware store or pharmacy that that astronauts in space can go visit for extra supplies (or bandages)!

ASTRONAUT AT WORK

NEIL ARMSTRONG

FAMOUS ASTRONAUTS

More than 530 people have traveled in space.

- Three completed a sub-orbital flight.
- Over 500 astronauts traveled to Earth orbit.
- Over twenty astronauts have gone beyond low-Earth orbit, including trips around the Moon.
- Twelve astronauts have walked on the Moon.
- Astronauts have spent over 29,000 days in space. Here are some of them:

Yuri Gagarin (Soviet Union) – the first man into space. He was a jet-fighter pilot before joining cosmonaut training in 1960. His flight was in 1961.

Valentina Tereshkova (Soviet Union) – was the first woman into space, in 1963, and orbited the Earth 48 times.

Neil Armstrong (United States) – may be the most famous astronaut of all. He was commander of the Apollo 11 mission to the Moon, and was the first human to walk on the Moon's surface. As he put his foot down on the dusty surface, Armstrong said, "That's one small step for a man; one giant leap for mankind."

NASA
ARMSTRONG

John Glenn (United States) – was the fifth person to leave Earth and the first American to orbit the Earth. After a long career as an astronaut, he went into politics and served in the United States Senate for 24 years.

James Lovell (United States) – was the first person to take part in four space missions. He traveled to the Moon twice, although he did not land there. He was commander of the Apollo 13 mission that suffered a critical failure on its way to the Moon. He, his crew, and the ground crew on Earth succeeded in bringing the mission home safely.

CHRIS HADFIELD

Chris Hadfield (Canada) – he watched the Apollo 11 mission landing in 1970 when he was nine, and determined to become an astronaut. He took part in several space missions, and in 2012 became the first Canadian commander of the ISS.

Hadfield is famous for using social media to explain life in space, and for performances on the ISS of songs like David Bowie's "Space Oddity". He is credited with raising profile of Earth's space programs among younger people, and in stimulating many people to apply to the astronaut program.

HADFIELD IN SPACE MISSION

BECOMING AN ASTRONAUT

Would you want to become an astronaut? It might be possible! Space agencies look for candidates with these qualities:

- Excellent health
- A background in science or technology
- Great team-working and personal skills
- A wide range of activities and experiences

However, just wanting to be an astronaut will not be enough. When Canada looked for new astronauts in 2016, it got thousands of applications. Almost 4,000 people passed the first screening, meaning they were technically qualified. After a year, that group of people was trimmed down to just two new astronauts.

JULIE PAYETTE
A CANADIAN ASTRONAUT

It is never too early to start on the health and knowledge parts! Regular exercise and eating well will move you toward great physical conditioning. Learning more, including from Baby Professor books like Where Does Outer Space Begin? and A Space Ride to Saturn, will help get you ready for all the knowledge an astronaut must gain.

See you among the stars!

Visit

www.BabyProfessorBooks.com

to download Free Baby Professor eBooks
and view our catalog of new and exciting
Children's Books